01

COMPUTER ANIMATION

NANCY DICKMANN

T0021587

KidHaven
PUBLISHING

Published in 2024 by
KidHaven Publishing, an Imprint of Greenhaven Publishing, LLC
2544 Clinton St., Buffalo, NY 14224

© 2023 Brown Bear Books Ltd

Text and Editor: Nancy Dickmann
Children's Publisher: Anne O'Daly
Design Manager: Keith Davis
Designer and Illustrator: Supriya Sahai
Picture Manager: Sophie Mortimer

Picture Credits
Key: t=top, b=bottom, c=center, l=left, r=right
Interior: Alamy: Jeff Morgan 06 25; Sueddeutsche Zeitung Photo 18. iStock: Gorodenkoff 20; hobo_18 5, 28.
Shutterstock: Mongkolchon Akesin 4; dangdumrong 22; diversepixel 10, 29t; FrameStockFootage 6, 7; Freedomz
23; Daniel Fung 19; Gaudi Lab 17; Kaspars Grinvalds 13; Iryna Imago 27; Tithi Luadthong 9, 29b; Marbella Studio
12, 15; Ovocim 16; Rido 27; Thawiwat Sae-Heng 11; Roman Samborskyi 14; Biserka Stojanovic 24; Twin Design 21.

Cataloging-in-Publication Data

Title: Computer animation / Nancy Dickmann.
Description: Buffalo, New York: KidHaven Publishing, 2024. |
Series: Cool computing jobs | Includes glossary and index.
Identifiers: ISBN 9781534546509 (pbk.) | ISBN 9781534546516 (library bound) | ISBN 9781534546523 (ebook)
Subjects: LCSH: Computer animation--Juvenile literature. |
Computer animation--Vocational guidance--Juvenile literature.
Classification: LCC TR897.7 D534 2024 | DDC 777'.7--dc23

Manufactured in the United States of America

CPSIA compliance information: Batch #CW24KH: For further information contact Greenhaven Publishing LLC at 1-844-317-7404.

Please visit our website, www.greenhavenpublishing.com.
For a free color catalog of all our high-quality books, call toll free 1-844-317-7404 or fax 1-844-317-7405.

Find us on

{ }

01

CONTENTS

MAKING MAGIC

Do you like watching movies? Have you ever wondered how they're made?

Movies and television shows can take us to another world—at least for a little while. Most are filmed with actors playing the parts, but others require more imagination. They might include talking animals or toys that come to life. That's where animation comes in!

A good movie can make you laugh, cry, or even jump in fear!

Drawn by Hand

Animated films have been around for more than 100 years. In the past, every frame was drawn by hand. Other films have used clay models that are moved a tiny bit at a time and filmed with a camera. Today, most animation is done on computers.

Making movies by moving models a little bit at a time is called stop-motion animation.

MORE THAN CARTOONS

We can't actually film movies in space, but CGI can make it look like actors are there.

You might have heard people talk about CGI in films. What does it mean?

Sometimes filmmakers can't tell the story they want using just actors and sets. That's where CGI comes in! It stands for "computer-generated imagery." That means images made by a computer. CGI is used in movies, television shows, and games.

No matter what CGI is used for, many of the jobs involved are the same.

What CGI Can Do

Computer animation is one use for CGI because it uses computers to create moving images. CGI can be used in other areas too. It can be used alongside shots of live actors. Computers can add backgrounds or make crowds look bigger.

CGI can also be used to add explosions. This is an example of visual effects, or VFX.

SETTING THE STYLE

Any CGI project starts with choosing a look. That's the job of a concept artist.

A concept artist will talk to the director about the idea for the movie. They will read the script if it's already written. Then, they come up with ideas for the overall look. What style will fit best? Will it be sleek and futuristic or brightly colored and silly?

A concept artist often works with a brief—a short description of the project.

Concept Art

Concept art is often done in 2D, even if the finished product will be 3D. These drawings set the mood for the project. They show what colors and shapes will be used. This art helps show the rest of the crew what the finished movie will look like.

Sometimes concept art is used like an ad, to try to convince a studio to fund a movie.

Concept art might be done with pencils or paints, or with computer drawing tools.

9

AN ANIMATED WORLD

CGI is used to create more than just characters. It can create the world they move in too.

In hand-drawn animation, characters are often drawn on clear plastic, then laid over a painted background. Even with computers, the background and characters are still created separately. The background is very important, though. It sets the scene.

A good background can make it feel like the action is really taking place on an alien planet.

Background Designer

A background designer creates the backgrounds. These must match the style of the animation. Background designers need to be creative and talented artists. For computer animation, they need to know how to use modeling software. It can create 3D shapes that look real.

Backgrounds need to be designed for games too. This job is often called an environment artist.

For live-action films, actors can be filmed in front of a green screen. A different background is added later.

CREATING CHARACTERS

Good characters can make a movie great. Their look is just as important as their actions.

A director or writer describes a character to a character designer. Is the character a person, an animal, or an alien? Are they silly, smart, sneaky, or scary? The character designer chooses a look to match the personality. They make sketches, either on paper or on a computer.

There are plenty of software tools to help character designers sketch out their ideas.

For some characters, the designer also has to think about what kind of clothes they will wear.

Character designers work closely with directors and writers to get the character's look just right.

Plenty of Options

The character designer produces lots of sketches. They show what the character will look like from different angles. They try to show the character's personality by using different poses and facial expressions. The animctors will use these sketches as a reference.

STORYBOARDS

A director wants to plan every shot in advance. They use a storyboard to do it.

When you write a story or report, you probably start with an outline. A storyboard is a kind of visual outline for a film. It looks like a comic strip. It shows where characters are positioned. It shows every camera angle and close-up.

If you are good at writing outlines, you might make a good storyboard artist!

Picturing a Story

A storyboard artist needs a good eye for what will look good on film. They want each shot to be interesting. For VFX, an artist takes a storyboard and turns it into a rough animation. They play the different shots in order to time out the scene.

Digital drawing software makes it easier to copy, edit, and change images that were drawn by hand.

Storyboard artists often use a stylus to draw on a laptop or tablet.

COMING TO LIFE

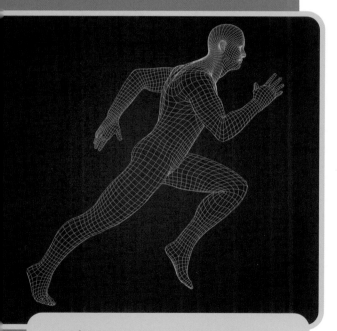

A wireframe shows a character's shape, but not their color or texture.

Animated characters don't stand still! They move around on screen. This process starts with a model.

A modeler studies the character design and uses special software to make a digital model. The model is 3D, but it doesn't look finished. It almost looks like it's made from chicken wire. That's why it's called a wireframe! It's a framework for the character.

Making It Move

Once the models are done, a rigger takes over. They make the character move by creating a rig. This is like a digital puppet version of the character. There might be different rigs for different body parts. They show how the character walks, waves, or smiles.

Modelers don't just create digital versions of characters. They also create model tools, weapons, and other objects.

Character designers check rigs to see if they match their idea of the character's movement.

{ }

ANIMATORS

Animators make still images Look Like they're moving. It's Like magic!

Moving pictures are an optical illusion. A movie is actually a sequence of still images, called frames. They swap so quickly that our brain interprets the picture as actually moving. For animated films, animators are in charge of making these still images.

Have you ever watched a picture "move" in a flip book? It tricks your brain just like a movie does.

Key Frames

Using rigs and 3D models, animators create the starting and ending points for certain scenes or shots. These are called key frames (or keyframes). Then, they go back and fill in the frames between them. Sometimes this is done by hand, but by using a rig, a computer can do the work instead.

Animators use many different types of software. Autodesk Maya is one of the most popular.

{ }

MOTION CAPTURE

Do you want to make an animated character move like a real person? Call an actor!

Some movies use a technique called motion capture, or mocap for short. An actor is filmed performing a scene. The actor wears a special skintight suit. It has little sensors on it—sometimes 30 or more! They track and record the actor's movements.

The sensors are placed on different parts of the body, such as arms and legs.

Animators have used motion capture while making the *Avatar* movies.

Time to Transform

Animators feed the sensor data into a computer. They use it to build a virtual "skeleton." Then, they animate it. They change the surface to make the actor look like an alien, a troll, or an animal. The character moves just like the real actor does.

Special motion capture scanners can capture an actor's facial expressions. This makes the finished version more realistic.

FINISHING TOUCHES

Texture artists might be inspired by natural textures, such as the scales on a snake's skin.

It's the little things that count when it comes to making an animated movie look good.

An animator is mainly concerned with pose and movement. Finalizing the look is a different job. A texture artist "paints" details onto the surface of an animated model. They can add fabric texture or creases, or put scratches or reflections on a car.

Seeing the Light

Directors use lighting to make actors look their best. In an animated movie, the lighting is added digitally. A lighting artist uses software to create the look they want. Is it sunny or cloudy? Is the scene lit by candlelight?

A good lighting design will make it clear where the light in a scene is coming from.

Lighting artists make color keys to show how each color will look in different light.

PUTTING IT ALL TOGETHER

All the parts of the movie are made. Now it's time to put them together!

A compositor creates the final images—the ones that the audience sees. They take the backgrounds, characters, and VFX that other people have made, and they put all the layers together. The goal is to make it look seamless.

When you watch a movie, you shouldn't be able to tell that all the parts were created separately.

A compositor needs a good eye for detail to make sure all the elements look right.

Making It Match

With VFX, a compositor often has to match CGI images to live footage of actors. There might be background images to add too. The compositor checks the lighting to make sure that everything matches. If it doesn't, the image might look fake.

A compositor might add shadows or a blurring effect on a moving object.

{ }

HOW TO PREPARE

Computer animation is a fun and creative career. It's never too early to start learning!

Some jobs in animation call for strong art skills. Practice your drawing whenever you can. Why not try out digital design tools? There are lots of free drawing apps available. You can even find ones that will let you animate the images you create.

Drawing apps have tools that let you easily color and edit your work.

Paying Attention

Other animation jobs need different skills. A storyboard artist needs a good eye for framing a shot. A rigger needs to understand how bodies move and be comfortable using animation software. A lighting artist needs to pay attention to color and details. Which skills do you have?

You might be able to find an online class to teach you computer animation.

Why not try making your own stop-motion movie using toys or models and a phone camera?

QUIZ

Which job in computer animation is the best fit for you? Answer these questions, and check your results at the end.

1. What kind of museum is your favorite?

A. An art museum—I like to look at amazing paintings.

B. A natural history museum—I love learning about animals and dinosaurs and seeing their skeletons.

C. Do they have comic book museums? Because that would be great!

2. When you're on vacation, how do you spend most of your time?

A. admiring the beautiful buildings and scenery

B. people watching

C. taking videos to send to my friends or post on social media

3. What's the main thing you use a computer for?

A. painting apps

B. playing games where I can build a world

C. watching movies

4. What's your favorite kind of book to read?

A. a sci-fi novel where I can read the descriptions and picture amazing alien worlds

B. anatomy textbooks (really!)

C. any kind of graphic novel

5. What would your friends say is your most impressive skill or trait?

A. my creativity

B. solving problems to figure out how to make something work

C. telling funny stories with lots of gestures and sound effects

Add up your answers.

What did you get?

Mostly As: You could be a concept artist, background designer, or character designer. You're creative, you have strong artistic skills, and you like to use your imagination.

Mostly Bs: You could be a modeler or rigger. You're interested in bodies and how they move, and you like building on a computer and solving problems.

Mostly Cs: You could be a storyboard artist. You like to draw and tell stories visually, and you understand how to use different shots for maximum impact.

GLOSSARY

computer-generated imagery (CGI) images created on a computer, which can be added to live action scenes or stand on their own

digital done electronically on a computer

director the person who decides how a movie will look on screen and tells the actors and crew what to do

frame one of the single images or photos that make up a film, forming the illusion of a moving image when they are shown quickly one after another

green screen a blank green background sometimes used when filming actors that is digitally replaced later with a different image

motion capture a way of electronically capturing the movement of a live actor and using it to create an animation

optical illusion something that tricks your eyes so that you think you see something different than what is actually there

script the written version of a movie, which includes the actors' lines and descriptions of scenes

sensor a device that detects or measures something such as heat, light, or movement

software programs for a computer

storyboard a visual outline for a film, showing what the different shots will look like

studio a company that makes movies and television programs

stylus a device like a pen that you can use to draw or write on a touch screen

texture the way that something feels when you touch it, for example rough or smooth

3D shown in three dimensions, so that it looks solid and has depth

2D shown in two dimensions, like a flat drawing

visual effects (VFX) the use of computer-generated imagery to create scenes in live-action movies that can't be filmed in real life

wireframe a digital skeleton for an animated character or object

FIND OUT MORE

Books

Lyons, Heather. *Programming Games and Animation.* Minneapolis, MN: Lerner Publishing Group, 2018.

Pagano, David, with David Pickett. *The LEGO Animation Book: Make Your Own LEGO Movies!* San Francisco, CA: No Starch Press, 2016.

Preuitt, Sheela. *20-Minute (Or Less) Animation Hacks.* Minneapolis, MN: Lerner Publishing Group, 2020.

Troupe, Thomas Kingsley. *Create Crazy Stop-Motion Videos.* Mankato, MN: Capstone Press, 2020.

Websites

This fascinating online exhibit shows how Pixar films are made:
sciencebehindpixar.org/explore

Discover more amazing facts about computer animation:
kids.kiddle.co/Computer_animation

Learn more about the different jobs involved in computer animation:
www.screenskills.com/job-profiles/browse/animation/

Go here for a detailed look at how computer animation works:
entertainment.howstuffworks.com/computer-animation.htm

Find tips and hints on making storyboards here:
www.canva.com/learn/how-to-build-a-storyboard/

INDEX